SWEDISH
Christmas
TRADITIONS

A Smörgåsbord of Scandinavian Recipes,
Crafts, and Other Holiday Delights

Ernst Kirchsteiger

Roland Persson ❄ Mia Gahne

Skyhorse Publishing

Ernst Kirchsteiger

Christmas isn't a competition; it's not as if the person who throws the best Christmas celebration wins. For me, Christmas is about something completely different.

We celebrate a pretty minimalist Christmas at my home in Ernstorp. We don't have all that many Christmas lights and decorations—but we have a lot of friends around. Of course, when you have people around, it's always fun to be able to offer them something nice to eat. Our fridge and cookie jars are fully stocked from the end of November.

To be able to just sit down and share a traditional ham sandwich and a beer with a good friend: that brings the spirit of Christmas to me. To have the time to relax, socialize, and just be a kid for a while.

I grew up as an ordinary immigrant kid in Degerfors, a blue-collar town. My mother was from Poland and my father from Austria. They did everything in their power to serve up impressive Christmas smörgåsbords every year. A big spread with traditional Swedish dishes was a sign that they had made it, even though they still bought two of everything because they were embarrassed not to know the correct words for "one" when they went shopping.

But my parents did something else for Christmas as well. They invited immigrant workers from the factories in town who hadn't been able to go home to their families and countries over the holidays. All of a sudden, I'd find myself at the Christmas table eating red cabbage with a rumbling old man with a wooden leg, the sort of person who had great stories to tell after a life spent sailing the seven seas.

I remember that as a child, I was incredibly proud of the fact that we opened our home to complete strangers. I've spent many Christmases working in mental institutions, seated on uncomfortable chairs, but still filled with the spirit of the holiday. And I've spent Christmas as a very nervous host on Swedish television—a benchmark in my career I'll always remember.

In other words, there's no right or wrong way to celebrate Christmas. That's what I want to show with this book. There is no "Christmas Police" that will come knocking on your door to judge if you've managed to pull off that picture-perfect Christmas. Do the holiday your own way.

I hope I can help you have a Christmas that's just right for you. It's all about focusing on the right things. Cut down on the expensive gifts; spend more time with the people you care about. You don't have to drive yourself crazy. It's not the number of decorations that are important, but their quality.

An honest Christmas lasts longer.

Ernst Kirchsteiger

Christmas Food

Christmas has its symbols: the Christmas tree, the presents and, last but not least, the food. In Sweden we're a little unusual with our special Christmas smörgåsbord laden with food. It's as if we want to prove that we can cook everything.

In Austria, where my father's family is from, people go to a restaurant for their Christmas meal. It ends up being just as cozy as cooking at home. I wish we could all relax like that, and not think about Christmas food in terms of strict, unchangeable traditions.

How many different kinds of pickled herring you make isn't important—what matters is which ones you end up serving. Quality rather than quantity is what matters. Start to think about the reasons behind why you make certain dishes. Maybe Grandma's sister loved the jellied veal, but she passed away ten years ago. . . . You might have been making the jellied veal for the last decade as a symbolic act, not because anyone actually eats it. Make the dishes that people actually like instead and you won't have as much to throw away afterwards.

My favorite Christmas food is fried pickled herring, so I always have a jar ready in the fridge around Christmastime. I also always have a couple of rolls of gingerbread dough ready in case people drop by for coffee, which happens all the time.

My Christmas food is quite traditional. I'm faithful to all the Swedish classics, but I like testing the boundaries and putting my own twist on things.

I'm lucky enough to live in a family of food lovers and I really enjoy cooking for them. There's no better spice for a cook than having people around who like your food.

Ernst's Apple Herring

A fresh and tart herring that is also easy on the eyes. The apples are a little unexpected, but add both taste and color. Note: Leave the peels!

You Need:

⅓ cup + 1½
   tablespoons vinegar,
   12%
¾ cup + 1½
   tablespoons sugar
1¼ cups water
about 20 whole grains of
   black pepper
1 bay leaf
3 rinsed herring filets
4 apples, Cox apples are
   the best
½ cup shredded leek, the
   green part

Boil the vinegar, sugar, water, pepper, and bay leaf until the sugar has dissolved completely. Allow to cool.

Slice the herring filets diagonally. Thinly chop the apples, without peeling them. Layer herring, apple, and leek in a glass jar. Pour in the vinegar marinade and leave for at least 5 hours.

"There's no better spice than being surrounded by people who like your food."

Crock-Pot Herring

Warm fish alternative to Jansson's Frestelse. Matjes herring is tasty as is, but it is divine when heated. The dish can be enjoyed next to the Christmas tree, or paired with new potatoes in a springtime lilac garden.

You Need:
- 1 large or 2 small red onions
- 2 cans of Matjes herring, 7 ounces each
- 8 hard-boiled eggs
- 1 large bunch of dill
- 4–5 tablespoons butter

Peel and slice the red onions. Cut the herring into diagonal pieces. Chop the eggs and the dill.

Layer herring, eggs, onion, and dill in an ovenproof Crock-Pot. Shave cold butter over the ingredients and place in the oven at 392°F for 8 minutes. It just needs warming up.

Serve with Vasterbotten cheese and crispbread.

Fried Pickled Herring

A must-have on my Christmas table. I love that these cheap ingredients come together to make what I consider a delicacy. Unsurprisingly, fried pickled herring is often served at the Kirchsteiger family's midsummer buffet as well.

You Need:

1 pound Baltic herring

2 eggs

¾ cup + 1½ tablespoons milk

about 1½ cups coarse rye flour

butter

oil

1 sliced red onion

20 black peppercorns

5 bay leaves

1 sliced carrot

Marinade:

⅓ cup + 1½ tablespoons vinegar, 12%

1 cup sugar

1¼ cups water

Cut the fins off the herring. Whisk together the eggs and the milk. Place the herring and the egg mixture in double plastic bags. Allow to marinate overnight.

Pour the rye flour onto a plate and turn the herrings in the flour. Heat the oil and butter in a frying pan. The temperature is right when the pan has stopped "talking" (when the butter has stopped making a hissing sound). Cook the herring in batches, allowing it to cool, and drain some of the excess liquid on some paper towels.

Boil the vinegar, sugar, and water until the sugar has dissolved. Allow to cool down.

Layer the herring filets, red onion, pepper, bay leaves, and carrot slices in a tall, clean glass jar. Pour in the vinegar mixture and allow to marinate for 1 to 2 days.

Tip: Enjoy for lunch paired with some boiled potatoes and a sauce made from sour cream, Dijon mustard, and some honey.

Christmas Fish Salad

A mild and gentle salad for the Christmas smörgåsbord. It's nice to eat some light white fish amidst all of the heavy food. A good alternative to shrimp salad and other slaws. By the way, dill is a wonderful herb.

You Need:
14 ounces white fish
1 cucumber
½ red onion
1 bunch of dill
¾ cup heavy cream
4 hard-boiled eggs
¾ cup sour cream
salt
pepper

Boil the fish, let it cool, and cut it into cubes. Peel the cucumber and cut it into sticks. Peel and finely chop the red onion. Chop the dill and whip the cream. Peel and chop the eggs.

Carefully mix the ingredients in a bowl. Add salt and pepper. Garnish with leftover dill and red onion.

"Fine home decoration smells like fried herring—my favorite food!"

Ernst's Quick Meatballs

If you need to make a lot of meatballs, it's worth piping rather than rolling them. With a bit of practice, you can pipe up to 200 in a really short period of time. I learned this trick when I was the chef at Grythyttans Inn.

You Need:

1 small yellow onion

1 1/3 cups milk

1/2 cup breadcrumbs

1 teaspoon white ground pepper

1 teaspoon ground allspice

1 tablespoon liquid honey

2 eggs

2 pounds mixed mincemeat

butter and/or oil for panfrying or greasing the pan

Peel and coarsely chop the onion. Blend the onion, milk, breadcrumbs, white pepper, allspice, honey, and eggs in a mixer. Fold in the mincemeat.

Pipe small balls of the meatball batter onto a greased baking pan. Cook in the oven at 437–482°F for about 8 to 10 minutes or until the meatballs have turned brown. They can also be panfried in butter or oil in batches.

Tip: The meatballs can be frozen on the pan when they've just been piped and put in plastic bags. Then, you can just take them out of the freezer and fry them before serving.

"Slowly but surely, the spirit of Christmas lowers itself on angel

wings over me. Finally, I feel Christmas in every fiber of my body."

Fresh Christmas Salad

Having a green salad for the buffet gives your guests the option to eat something other than sausages, meat, and ham.

You Need:
2 containers arugula
¾ cup shelled hazelnuts
2 pears
1 pomegranate
Vasterbotten cheese, to
    taste

Dressing:
1 squeezed orange
1 tablespoon white
    balsamic vinegar
½ cup + 1½ tablespoons
    cold-pressed canola oil
1 teaspoon liquid honey
salt
freshly ground pepper

Carefully rinse the arugula and let it lie in cold water for a while. Take it out of the water and dry it off—nobody likes droopy salad leaves . . .

Roast the hazelnuts in a pan or in the oven. Note: Roasting nuts in the oven can be tricky. First nothing happens at all and then everything happens at once, so don't leave the kitchen. Then use a kitchen towel to rub off their skins.

Cut the pears into pieces. Take the pomegranate apart and pick out the seeds, making sure you leave the white parts behind. Crumble the cheese into smallish parts. Mix pears, nuts, arugula, and cheese. Sprinkle on the pomegranate seeds—they're so pretty they should be at the top.

Whip together the dressing and wind it over the salad. Leftover dressing can be poured into a bottle and refrigerated.

Ernst's Best Ham Glaze

This glaze is fantastic because it stays on the ham and doesn't fall off like a lot of other glazes do. Rosemary is one of my favorite herbs—it tastes like a meeting of the Mediterranean and Northern Sweden.

You Need:

1 Christmas ham, pre-cooked or grilled
⅓ cup chopped fresh rosemary (or ¾ cup dried)
⅓ cup mustard
5 tablespoons sugar
2 eggs
¾ cup–1¼ cups breadcrumbs

Garnish:

extra rosemary, preferably with hard stalks

Cut away the top layer of fat on the ham, leaving about ½ inch. The fat contributes a lot of flavor, so if you don't want to eat it, cut it off on your plate later on.

Chop the rosemary if you're using fresh herbs. Mix the mustard, sugar, eggs, and rosemary. Add enough breadcrumbs for the mixture to not be too messy.

Pat the mixture onto the ham, making a thin coating. Place the ham in a pan or an ovenproof mold. Grill it in the middle of the oven at 482°F for 15 minutes or until the glaze has turned a nice color.

Garnish with fresh sprigs of rosemary.

Kirchsteiger's Coarse Christmas Mustard

This super-quick and really tasty mustard is the perfect complement to the Christmas ham. Thank goodness for the hand mixer! It really is one of my best friends in the kitchen. In the old days, mustard was made using a cannonball rolled in a bowl you'd hold between your knees.

You Need:

1½ tablespoons yellow mustard seeds (double the amount for a stronger mustard)
6 tablespoons water
⅓ cup + 1½ tablespoons white balsamic vinegar
1 teaspoon salt
3–4 teaspoons honey
3 tablespoons canola oil

Blend the mustard seeds, water, balsamic vinegar, salt, honey, and oil in a saucepan or a bowl.

Mix with the hand mixer and taste. Serve with the Christmas ham.

Tip: If the mustard becomes too thick after swelling for a while, stir in some water.

Traude's Red Cabbage

My mother Traude made the best red cabbage in the neighborhood. Her reputation grew, and within a few years, she was cooking red cabbage for half of Degerfors. Apples are exciting to cook with—anyone who has ever eaten an apple has experienced its combination of sweetness, sourness, and special texture.

You Need:

2 pounds red cabbage

5 Cox apples

1 onion

5 whole cloves

3 grains of allspice

1 tablespoon butter

1¼ cups water

2 cubes of meat stock

3–4 tablespoons vinegar, 12%

2 tablespoons black currant cordial, undiluted

3 tablespoons honey

Thinly slice the red cabbage—you can use a cheese slicer for this. Core the apples and cut them into thin slices. Peel and chop the onion. Grind the cloves and the allspice with a mortar and pestle.

Heat the butter in a large saucepan, and let the apples and onion heat up for a while without browning. Add the red cabbage and the water. Stir and add the spices, stock, vinegar, cordial, and honey.

Cook on low heat under a lid until the cabbage has gone limp, about 20 minutes. Add honey to taste if you want the cabbage sweeter, or vinegar for more tartness.

Tip: Can be made into a great red cabbage slaw if you add whipped cream; better than all the beetroot salads in the world.

Pickled Vegetables

An alternative for people who don't like pickled herring. Put the whole jar on the table to add some color to the Christmas spread.

You Need:

3 carrots

2 parsnips

1 small fennel

½ cauliflower head

1 tree of broccoli

1 yellow onion

Marinade:

1¼ cups water

¾ cup + 1½ tablespoons
  sugar

⅓ cup + 1½ tablespoons
  vinegar or white
  wine vinegar

5 star anise seeds

1 stick of cinnamon

1 bay leaf

Boil the marinade with the spices until the sugar has dissolved.

Peel the carrots and the parsnips and slice them into dime-sized pieces. Cut the fennel into wedges. Divide the cauliflower and broccoli into bouquets. Peel the onion and cut it into wedges. Layer all of the vegetables in a well-cleaned glass jar. Pour in the warm marinade and seal the jar. Refrigerate for at least 24 hours before serving.

Glazed Ribs

My sons love ribs, so I always have them on our Christmas table. I learned the trick of boiling the ribs before grilling them from a Turkish woman who prepared lamb that way. It's a good technique for summer barbeques as well.

You need:

2 pounds thick or thin ribs,
*   according to your taste*
1 onion, in wedges
3 bay leaves
20 peppercorns
1 carrot, sliced

Glaze:

⅓ cup + 1½ tablespoons
*   honey*
2 tablespoons soy sauce
1 teaspoon salt
1 teaspoon ground white
*   pepper*
1½ teaspoons ground
*   ginger*
2 tablespoons olive oil

Put the ribs in a large pot with the onion, bay leaves, peppercorn, and carrot with enough water to cover the meat. Boil until the meat feels tender, about 1 hour. Drain and place in an ovenproof mold or a roasting pan.

Melt the honey and mix with soy sauce, salt, white pepper, ginger, and olive oil. Coat the ribs with the glaze and grill in the oven at 392°F for about 10 minutes. Don't be afraid to brush on some more glaze toward the end of the grilling.

My Best Liver Pâté

Not for people who don't like the taste of liver, but chicken liver has a mild and delicate flavor. My pâté is great with a little bit of cucumber. I like eating it on a piece of rye bread when I come back from church on Christmas morning.

You Need:

13 ounces chicken liver
3 ounces minced pork
2 boiled potatoes
¼ onion, finely chopped
2 salted, tinned sprats
1 egg
2½ tablespoons wheat
    flour
2½ teaspoons salt
1 teaspoon white pepper
1¼ cups heavy cream
2 tablespoons olive oil +
    some extra for the mold
1–2 tablespoons cognac

Chop the liver into small pieces, then put it with the other ingredients into a food processor. Mix into a smooth batter. Grease 1 large or 2 small ovenproof molds with olive oil. Bake at 300°F for 70–80 minutes. Test that the pâté is ready by sticking it with a toothpick—if the juices are clear, it's done. Allow to cool.

"I'm not a glitter person.
Too much glitter everywhere makes too much of a fuss."

Ernst's Delicious Christmas Bread

A fine tasting and easy-to-make loaf which doesn't need to rise and lasts a long time. Excellent with a strong cheese, or served with a slice of Christmas ham.

You need:

3 cups wheat flour

1¼ cups graham flour

¾ cup + 1½ tablespoons
   coarse rye flour

2 teaspoons salt

2 teaspoons bicarbonate of
   soda

¾ cup + 1½ tablespoons
   treacle

4¼ cups plain yogurt

¾ cup raisins

¾ cup whole hazelnuts

1¼ cups dried, shredded
   apricots

butter for the pans

¾ cup sunflower or
   pumpkin seeds

Mix all of the flour, salt, and bicarbonate of soda in a stainless steel mixing bowl. Add treacle, yogurt, raisins, nuts, and apricots.

Grease 2 rectangular bread pans and cover them with sunflower seeds or pumpkin seeds.

Scrape the sticky dough into the pans, making sure to leave about 1 inch of space to the rim to give the dough room to rise. Even out the surface and sprinkle on some extra sunflower and/or pumpkin seeds.

Bake at 392°F for 60 minutes, then lower the temperature to 347°F and bake for another 30 minutes. Turn the loaves over onto a grate and allow to cool.

Tip: Great present. Wrap the loaf in a new, clean kitchen towel and you have a great Christmas gift.

"I think apricots have such a beautiful color. They're almost sensual."

Ernst's Rosemary Crispbread

Nothing is as attractive and tasty as your own homemade crispbread. Don't worry about trying to get it perfect—it should show that it's handmade.

About 20 pieces
4 tablespoons yeast
2 cups lukewarm water
3–4 teaspoons salt
4¼ cups coarse rye flour
2 cups wheat flour
1 tablespoon dried
　rosemary

Crumble the yeast into a bowl and dissolve in the lukewarm water. Add salt, rye flour, wheat flour, and rosemary. Knead into a smooth dough. Let rise under a kitchen towel until the dough reaches double its original size. This takes about 1 to 2 hours.

Roll out the dough with a regular rolling pin to a thin pancake, about ¹⁄₁₆ inch thick. Cut out round shapes with a small plate or something similar and roll them with a kruskavel, a knobbly rolling pin, or prick the dough with a fork. You can also place the entire dough pancake in a pan covered with baking paper, roll over it with the kruskavel, and break it into pieces after it has been baked.

Bake on a baking paper-covered pan at 482°F for about 15 minutes.

Tip: Try it with sage or fennel instead of rosemary. This crispbread is also great to bake covered with parmesan or Vasterbotten cheese, and served in small pieces as a cocktail snack.

Liptauer

This lovely Austrian fromage frais is a slightly unusual addition to the Christmas table. It's great as a garnish or on a sandwich. The recipe makes a large batch, but in Austria people are fond of big dinners, perhaps a throwback from the Second World War. Warning: Mildly addictive.

You Need:

1 yellow onion
2 garlic cloves
5 hard-boiled eggs
1¾ cups fromage frais, 10% fat
13 tablespoons butter
1 teaspoon salt
½ teaspoon white pepper
1½ tablespoons Dijon mustard
1 teaspoon paprika
1 tablespoon white balsamic vinegar

Peel the onion, garlic, and eggs. Put all of the ingredients in a bowl or a food processor and mix well.

Serve as a garnish with food or on bread.

"Not having salt in your bread is about as interesting as kissing your sister on Midsummer's Eve; absolutely nothing happens."

Ulla's Grandma's Oat Crackers

My wife Ulla makes these crackers. Her grandfather had the first big grocery store in Degerfors, so these crackers may well have showed up on local coffee tables back in the day. This recipe is probably at least a hundred years old—and it's still good today.

Makes 20–30 crackers

5 tablespoons porridge
 oats
1½ cups + 1½
 tablespoons wheat flour
16 tablespoons (2 sticks)
 butter
1¼ cups sugar
1 cup half and half
1½ teaspoons
 bicarbonate of soda

Mix all the ingredients and knead into dough. Let the dough sit for an hour.

Roll out the dough to about ¼-inch thickness. Use the bottom of a grater to cut out rectangular shapes.

Place on a pan covered with baking paper and bake at 347°F for about 10 minutes or until the crackers are golden brown.

Tip: Stack 10–15 crackers and tie a pretty ribbon around them. In an instant, you have the perfect gift to bring the hosts of a mulled wine party.

Orange-Flavored Shortbread

Their slightly unexpected flavor goes well with a cup of tea. Citrus flavors always make me think of Christmas.

Makes about 50
32 tablespoons (4 sticks)
    unsalted butter
1½ cups cane sugar
2 oranges
2 eggs
4¼ cups wheat flour
½ teaspoon salt

Whisk the butter and sugar until fluffy. Wash the oranges, grate their rinds, and add to the mixture. Whisk one egg at a time. Mix the flour and salt and add the mixture to the batter. Blend well.

Cover the dough and leave in the fridge for about 2 hours. Roll it out on flour-coated baking paper to a rectangle about 12 × 16 inches. Put it on a baking pan and bake for about 30 minutes at 347°F in the middle of the oven. Take it out and cut it into squares while the pan is warm. Allow to cool.

Tip: If the dough becomes too hard in the fridge, cut it into smaller pieces and leave it at room temperature for a while.

"Walking across a floor that you know people have used for 200 years means a lot more to me than having a central vacuum cleaner."

Saffron Pancake

The crowning glory of my Christmas table. I make it instead of Swedish cheesecake or rice cream desserts every Christmas. Serving this bright yellow dish in a black cast-iron mold makes it even more attractive.

You need:
1 packet saffron
½ teaspoon salt
3 eggs
1¾ cups milk
⅓ cup sugar
2 pounds rice pudding

For serving:
lightly whipped heavy
   cream
cherry preserves

Pound the saffron and salt in a mortar. Mix the eggs, milk, and sugar into a batter. Add the rice pudding and the salt-saffron blend. Stir carefully.

Pour the batter into a buttered ovenproof mold and cook at 347–392°F or until the batter has solidified.

Serve with lightly whipped heavy cream and cherry preserves. Can be eaten cold or at room temperature.

Cardamom Mumma Drink

This variation of mumma, an old-fashioned Swedish drink, can be just the thing to take your dinner party to the next level. This is my way of adding some variety to the traditional Swedish Christmas beverages like seasonal beers and soft drinks; I love the taste of cardamom.

You Need:
2 teaspoons cardamom
*   seeds*
¼–½ cup sugar
*   (according to taste)*
1¼ cups Madeira
2 bottles of port
2 bottles of Christmas beer

Pound the cardamom seeds with a little of the sugar in a mortar. Mix this and the rest of the sugar into the Madeira. Mix so that the sugar dissolves and leave it for a while. Decant into a pretty jug. Pour in the port and beer just before serving so there's a lot of foam left.

"Christmas has many colors. Who says it needs to be red? Blue and white Christmas trees are too rare in this country."

Almond and Vanilla Milk

Warm winter treat, perfect after a cold day outdoors.

For 2 glasses
1 vanilla pod
2 cups milk
1 tablespoon syrup or
   honey
½ cup peeled and skinned
   almonds
1 teaspoon vanilla sugar

Score the vanilla pod with a sharp knife. Scrape out the seeds and pour them with the milk into a saucepan. Bring to a boil. Take off the stove and allow to steep for a while.

Carefully reheat. Add the rest of the ingredients and blend with the hand mixer until smooth. Serve warm.

Ernst's Fried Wild Boar

A fun way to make 3-D piggies, which kids usually enjoy. Make sure you're careful with the hot oil, though.

Makes 20–30
10½ tablespoons butter
2 cups milk
3½ tablespoons yeast
⅔ cup sugar
about 6 cups wheat flour
4¼ cups vegetable oil,
*   such as sunflower oil*

For Decoration:
1 cup sugar
2 tablespoons cinnamon

Melt the butter in a saucepan, add the milk, and heat until it reaches body temperature (98°F).

Crumble the yeast in a bowl and mix in sugar and salt. Pour in the heated liquids.

Add the flour, saving some for rolling out the dough. Allow to rise under a kitchen towel for about 30 minutes.

Roll out the dough on a flour-covered surface, to about ½-inch thickness. Use a cookie cutter to make pig shapes.

Cut slits in the legs and ears.

Heat the oil in a thick-bottomed saucepan. Try with a ball of dough to see if the oil is hot enough. When the dough ball turns golden brown, start deep-frying a few pigs at a time. Have a lid handy in case the oil gets too hot.

Drain the oil from the pigs by putting them on a paper towel.

Mix sugar and cinnamon in a bowl. Roll the pigs in the mixture. Yummy!

Walnut and Saffron Crisp Rolls

The whole house is filled with the scent of saffron when you bake these crisp rolls. Saffron and walnuts are a great combination. We usually bake these around St. Lucia Day (December 13th), put them in a cookie jar in the kitchen, and tell ourselves that they'll last until Christmas. They always run out, and we end up baking a second batch.

Makes 40–50

1 cup walnuts
7 tablespoons butter
3 eggs
1 cup sugar
1 pinch saffron
½ teaspoon salt
2½–3 cups wheat flour
1 teaspoon baking powder

Chop the nuts coarsely. Melt the butter in a pot and let cool. Whisk the eggs and sugar until fluffy. Pound the saffron with salt in a mortar and add to the butter. Combine the nuts, flour, and baking powder in a separate bowl and then mix them with the saffron butter and the egg butter to make a fairly loose dough.

Split the dough into 3 parts and shape them into oblong rolls. Add more flour if the dough feels too loose. Place the rolls on a baking paper-covered pan. Bake at 392°F for about 20 minutes. Diagonally slice the rolls to make crisp rolls. Dry in the oven at 167°F for 60 minutes. Store in an airtight container.

Cumin Cookies

Tasty lady-shaped cookies that also aid your digestion. Cumin is a fun and unusual spice to use in pastries.

Makes 20–30
¾ cup granulated sugar
13 tablespoons soft butter
1 egg
2 cups wheat flour
*2 tablespoons ground
    cumin*

Stir the sugar and butter until it is light. Mix in the egg, flour, and cumin. Knead to a soft dough. Roll out on a floured table.

Make girl shapes with a cookie cutter and place on a baking paper-covered pan. Bake at 392°F for 5 to 7 minutes.

Ulla's Cut Gingerbread

We keep a couple rolls of dough in the fridge for unexpected guests. As soon as someone rings the doorbell, we'll just cut off a few slices and bake them. It's relaxing not to always have to take out the rolling pin and make gingerbread men. There's beauty in simplicity.

Makes about 150

14 tablespoons butter

½ cup + 1½ tablespoons syrup

1 cup sugar

grated rind from 1 lemon

1 tablespoon ground cinnamon

½ tablespoon ground cloves

½ tablespoon ground ginger

½ tablespoon cardamom

½ teaspoon bitter Seville orange rind

about 3 cups wheat flour

¾ tablespoon bicarbonate of soda

¼ cup almonds, scalded and finely chopped

For Decoration

whole almonds, blanched

Pour the butter, syrup, and sugar into a saucepan. Heat them slowly on the lowest temperature and stir until the butter has completely melted. Let cool.

Add the lemon rind and the spices. Mix the flour, bicarbonate of soda, and almonds. Work into the sugar and butter batter.

Quickly knead the dough smooth and make 2 rolls, about 2 inches in diameter. Wrap in plastic film and refrigerate overnight.

Slice thinly, less than ¼ inch thick, place on a baking paper-covered pan and bake for 7 minutes at 392°F.

If you like, put an entire blanched almond in the center of each cookie before baking.

Tip: Great with a bit of blue cheese, especially when served with glögg (Swedish mulled wine).

Divine Cinnamon Hearts

Great old-fashioned-tasting cookies. Cinnamon is always a safe bet during the Christmas season.

Makes 20–30
½ cup sugar
14 tablespoons butter
about 1⅔ cups flour
about 1 cup vanilla sauce
*   mix (1 packet makes*
*   7 portions)*

For Decoration
1 egg
2 teaspoons cinnamon
2 tablespoons sugar

Mix the sugar and butter to a white, light batter—an electric whisk is great for this. Add flour and vanilla sauce mix and knead to a smooth dough. Leave in the fridge for about 30 minutes.

Roll out to a thin layer, about ¹⁄₁₂–¼ inch thick. Use a cookie cutter to make heart shapes. Paint over the shapes with whipped egg. Mix the cinnamon and sugar and dip the cookies in the mixture. Place on a baking paper-covered pan and bake at 392°F for 6 to 8 minutes or until the cookies are a nice color.

Ernst's Favorite White Truffles

Incredibly tasty and pretty truffles that melt in your mouth. A must for the candy lover!

Makes about 20
1⅓ cups white chocolate
½ cup heavy cream
⅔ cup marzipan
3½ tablespoons butter
1 tablespoon white port

Garnish:
½ cup icing sugar
½ cup granulated sugar

Melt the chocolate and cream at low temperatures. Remove the pot from stove. Grate marzipan over it and stir it in with butter and port.

Pour the paste into a mold and place it in the snow or the freezer until the paste thickens enough to be shaped into balls.

Mix the icing sugar and granulated sugar. Roll the balls in the sugar mixture.

Christmas Music

Music is incredibly important if you want the angels of Christmas to appear and it's a great way to get in the spirit of things. I'm a music addict—very few moments pass when I'm not surrounded by music. Music is like my mental support wheel—it's easy to fall without it.

Ernst's Best Christmas Music

Christmas With My Friends—Nils Landgren

A fellow Degerfors person whom I've liked for a long time. A slightly fresher take on classic Christmas songs.

"Music is like my mental support wheel—it's easy to fall without it."

Candied Apples

Great showpieces on the dessert table, they are both good to eat and serve as decorations. Attractive, healthy, and unhealthy, all at the same time.

You Need:

1¼ cups sugar

1 tablespoon glucose (can also use clear syrup)

5 drops red food coloring

5 teaspoons water

5 twigs or skewers

5 small red apples

1 cup grated coconut

Boil sugar, glucose, food coloring, and water until the mixture has caramelized. Test this by pouring a drop into a glass of water. If the drop hardens, it's ready.

Poke the twigs into the apples and dip the apples into the heated syrup. Pour the grated coconut on a plate and roll the apples in it. Place on a plate and let solidify.

Chocolate and Peanut Candy

I like making candy that serves many people. This kind is pretty easy to make.

Makes 40

1 can of peanut butter

¾ cup + 1½ tablespoons
  syrup

⅓ cup + 1½ tablespoons
  sugar

4¼ cups Kellogg's
  Special K

1 teaspoon vanilla sugar

For Glazing

½ cup dark chocolate

½ cup light chocolate
  (optional)

Melt the peanut butter, syrup, and sugar in a saucepan. Add the Special K and vanilla sugar.

Pour the batter into a greased pan and flatten. Let harden in the fridge.

Chop the chocolate and melt it carefully without mixing, either in the microwave or in a water bath. Decorate in a pattern of your choosing.

Cut into pieces and store in the fridge or the freezer.

Tip: Can be deep-frozen and served directly when guests stop by for coffee.

Marzipan Medallions

A bit sticky to make but worth the effort. Great with coffee.

Makes 30–35
2¼ cups marzipan
½ cup walnuts
½ cup pistachios
2–3 tablespoons cognac
    (optional, but a shame
    to leave out . . .)
⅔ cup white chocolate

Mix the marzipan with the chopped walnuts, pistachios (save some nuts for decoration), and cognac. Roll into a round sausage, which is then sliced in ½ inch-thick pieces. Put the slices on a pan and refrigerate for an hour.

Melt white chocolate in the microwave or in a water bath. Paint with or dip the medallions in the chocolate. Decorate with walnuts and pistachios.

Tip: You can also make a large loaf of marzipan that you slice like bread.

"I try to avoid people who suck energy. Out with the vampires and in with the cotton wool people."

Toffee in the Microwave

Nice and easy way of making toffee, which saves you from burning your fingers having to pour the hot batter into tiny molds. I think it's much more fun than small and picky sophisticated candies.

You need:
1/2 cup heavy cream
3/4 cup sugar
1/2 cup syrup
3/4 cup roasted cashews
1/3 cup roasted hazelnuts
1/3 cup walnuts
1 tablespoon butter

Mix the cream, sugar, and syrup in a microwave-safe bowl. Microwave at top heat for 10–12 minutes. Test the batter by pouring a drop into cold water. When it's ready, you should be able to roll it into a hard marble.

Add nuts and butter and stir carefully. Spread the batter on a baking paper. Allow it to harden. Break into pieces and store in the fridge.

Flaming wine

The best party trick! The pretty flames cheer everyone up; no one can resist the mysterious blue flame. It turns into the best glögg ever. Warning: Tipsiness may follow.

You need:
2 bottles red wine
2 sticks of cinnamon
2 inches fresh ginger or
*   1 dried piece*
1 dried Seville orange rind
20 cardamom seeds or
*   5–6 whole capsules*
5–6 star anise seeds
1½ cups vodka
1 small sugarloaf (look for
*   this in specialty stores,*
*   stock up)*

Heat the wine and spices for about 5 minutes, enough time for the spices to flavor the wine. Do not let it come to a boil. Add the liquor and heat for another 5 minutes, being careful that it does not boil.

Take the saucepan outside. Cover about half of the saucepan with a grate and place the sugarloaf on the grate. Ladle the warm glögg over the sugarloaf. Set fire to the liquid. Continue ladling the burning glögg over the sugarloaf until the sugar has completely dissolved.

Serve your cheering guests!

The Spices of Christmas

Traditional Christmas spices are an important part of setting the mood, not least because of their wonderful scents. Gingerbread smells incredible when you're baking it, but really, the smell is from the spices. I also like to use whole spices as decorations.

Cinnamon – A piece of dried bark from the cinnamon tree that is attractive in pot-pourri and pickles, and is also a ground spice integral to many of the baked goods served at Christmas, as well as on top of the white Christmas rice porridge.

Seville Orange Rind – Gives a grown-up citrus flavor to the glögg (mulled wine) and is nice when ground in certain pastries, salad dressings, etc.

Star anise – Quite new to the Swedish kitchen, but has quickly become popular. It is good in glögg and pickling; it gives a complex taste reminiscent of licorice. It is incredibly beautiful as a table decoration.

Cloves – A natural part of gingerbread and various pickles. They are an ancient spice in the Swedish kitchen. According to old wives' tales, cloves help soothe toothaches. The combination of oranges and cloves is an icon of Swedish Christmas.

Cardamom – Can basically be used instead of cinnamon for a new and unexpected flavor. Cardamom buns are new favorites that are here to stay. A fresh fruit salad in syrup boiled with cardamom seeds is a wonderful combination of flavors.

Christmas Flowers

I love flowers. For me, it's not Christmas if I don't have amaryllis and hyacinths blooming. Flowers are so much more than colors and interesting shapes: they are living creatures that you have to take care of.

Their perishability appeals to me. They have a peak and then they die. We are forced to accept that not everything lasts forever and that some things must be allowed to take time. Planting a tulip bulb and knowing that you have to wait until next year to see it bloom—that sort of patience both teaches you life lessons and lowers your blood pressure.

Unfortunately, Christmas flowers can often be a little shy. Flowers are at their best when they're just bunched together. It's not always the most expensive flower arrangements that give the strongest impressions. A couple of blue hyacinths in a rusty tin jar can be so much better. There's beauty in simplicity—in all parts of life.

Flowers paired with fruit, citrus as well as apples, give a fun feeling around Christmas. Feel free to add something else edible, like whole spices, nuts, or red onions.

I have a lot of gardeners in my family. Perhaps that's why I often find myself seated under my fig tree. That's where I'm the happiest.

If people thought it was as natural to bring home flowers as a bottle of wine on Friday nights, we'd have a much more pleasant and beautiful society.

Hyacinths in Glasses

Hyacinths have a clean, tidy Christmas smell, a thousand times better than any perfume store. A nice way of showing them off is in old-fashioned hyacinth glasses, as the roots themselves are very pretty. Traditionally, you'd grow them in the actual glasses, but this is a way of cheating your way to the same result.

You need:

3 white or blue hyacinths

3 hyacinth glasses (look in flower shops or home decorating stores)

Carefully remove as much soil as possible from the roots. Rinse away the rest of the soil. Place a hyacinth in each of the glasses, making sure all the roots are in the glass. Fill with water to the bottom of the bulb.

So simple and incredibly beautiful.

Christmas Roses in a Bucket

The delicate Christmas rose looks great in a simple bucket and can be nicely complemented by vines. Moss- and lichen-covered twigs from the forest give a wintry feel and offer a contrast to all of the lines. The Christmas rose is a really important flower for me; its discrete charm is a symbol for the Virgin Mary. And, of course, it's wonderful that it decides to bloom while the ground is still covered with snow.

You Need:

Leca balls

1 old bucket, such as zinc
*   or enamel*

soil

2 Christmas roses

2 vines

possibly moss

3 twigs from nature,
*   preferably covered in*
*   moss*

Cover the bottom of the bucket with Leca balls. Fill it up with soil and plant the Christmas roses and vines. Cover the surface with moss if you have some. Place twigs here and there.

This arrangement looks wonderful on your front porch in nice weather. As it's in a bucket, it's easy to move in and out of the house.

Mistletoe Bouquet

The mistletoe is a legendary plant that makes us kiss, which is always nice. Even the ancient druids used to use it in their love potions. A good way of keeping it alive is using it as a cut flower. If you hang it upside-down it just dries up and looks a little dull. It works just as well as a symbol of kissing if it's standing on the table.

You Need:
1 mistletoe
1–2 red or white amaryllis,
  cut
low vase, preferably glass
1 wooden skewer
1 red onion

Undo the bunch of mistletoe. Cut the amaryllis to about the same length as the mistletoe. Place in a pretty vase filled with cold water. Drive the skewer into the onions and place low, close to the flowers.

Sideways Amaryllis

The simplest arrangements are often the most beautiful. Sometimes, it's fun to do something a little unexpected. Flowers should be "conversation pieces" at the dinner table. People are guaranteed to talk about this bouquet, I promise.

You Need:
2 white or red amaryllis, cut
1 pretty elongated bowl, such
* as an old kneading trough*
apples

Cut the amaryllis stems anew. Fill the trough with apples and place the flowers on top in a decorative way.

The flowers are then watered directly into the "tubes." Place them in a regular case when the dinner is over.

" *Being artistic is both a blessing and a curse. You can't let anything ugly be left alone.* "

Winter Chard

I found this chard at home in my flowerbed and thought it deserved a second chance. Perhaps you have something in your garden that has withstood the winter and is worth bringing inside. You don't always have to buy new things.

You Need:

1 plant from outside, such as a stand of chard

soil

1 flowerpot, preferably a little worn

moss

red onion

Carefully dig up your outdoor plant and plant it with soil in a suitable pot. Cover the surface with moss. Decorate with the red onion.

A simple plant like this gives me so much more than a huge bunch of roses.

Christmas Tulips on a Citrus Hill

I think planting some Christmas tulips is worth the effort. They're so cute and look almost like little gnomes. Also, they're great for putting on the table as they're so low. Many people make the mistake of having flowers that are too tall—but then you can't see your guests.

You Need:

low container, such as a cake mold, fruit bowl, or an old wash bowl

soil

10 Christmas tulips with bulbs

moss

5 kumquats

twigs from nature

possibly rosehips or dried rowan berries

Fill the container with soil, shape into a hill, and press the tulips down so they are stable. Cover the surface with moss. Decorate with kumquats and a few small twigs.

Wintry discoveries from the forest, like rosehips or rowan berries, can be great additions.

Water the tulips inside the "skirt," in the actual leaves, so they have the strength to develop in an interesting way.

Wormwood with Amaryllis

Sometimes you don't even have to plant the flowers. It's enough just to place a couple of different kinds to make them seem new and fresh. Frosty, silvery wormwood matched with white amaryllis make wintry poetry.

You Need:

1 pot or 1 bunch of
   wormwood
2 white amaryllis
1 large flower pot or vase

Here it's the combination that does the trick. Place the amaryllis in the midst of the wormwood, either in the middle of different pots or as cut flowers.

Christmas Decorations

For me, I find beauty in the irregular. When something's a little bushy, straggly, lopsided, or crooked it becomes beautiful. This is as true of people as of Christmas wreaths. That's why I prefer to make my Christmas decorations myself. There's nothing wrong with buying new ones, but perhaps you can make the effort to add something personal. It can be something the kids made at preschool that they're now really embarrassed about.

As is often the case, the simplest is the prettiest. I like materials from nature—lichen-covered twigs, dried rosehips, lingonberry sprigs, and branches of pine. Go for a hike in the forest to find supplies rather than becoming a regular at the decoration store.

Red apples, citrus fruits, and whole spices are also part of Christmas. Often, you can eat half of our decorations, and the rest go into the compost. That way, we don't have to pack and unpack our decorations every year.

Unfortunately, ugly Christmas lights are disfiguring Sweden and we seem to buy more of them every year. I don't understand why. A simple green Christmas tree with the most basic outdoor lighting is much better at bringing Christmas spirit than a twinkling polar bear lantern.

And you shouldn't forget the great feeling of lighting your own snow lantern.

Bird Candy

Birds need candy in the winter, too. Be compassionate and make them a yummy and good meal. At the same time, you get a pretty decoration for your garden.

You Need:
3 cups coconut fat
⅔ cup chopped nuts (any kind)
⅔ cup birdseed
string
cookie cutters

Melt the coconut fat and stir in the chopped nuts and seeds. Let cool to a thick porridge. Pour the batter into a pan, put a string into it, make a shape using a cookie cutter (such as a heart or a star), and allow to harden. Hang in a tree.

"We only have our homes for a short while. It's important to show them respect by loving them endlessly."

Improvised Christmas Tree

You don't have to buy an entire Christmas tree. Make your own improvised miniature version that can be kept either inside or outside. This makes a dense and stable fir whose shape you can adjust.

You Need:
1 flowerpot
soil
6–10 birch branches
wire
sprigs of fir, juniper, and/or
 pine
possibly red apples
possibly wooden skewers

Fill the pot with soil. Place the birch branches around the perimeter.

Pull the branches together at the top and wrap wire around the top. Insert fir sprigs from the base all the way up.

If you want to, you can string up apples on a wire (or wooden skewers) and insert them here and there. You can also wind a garland of Christmas lights around the "tree."

Tip: Make 2 and place 1 on either side of your front door. They are fine in any weather and are pretty lit with Christmas lights.

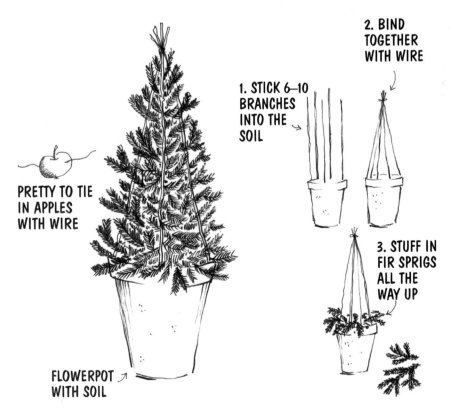

PRETTY TO TIE IN APPLES WITH WIRE

FLOWERPOT WITH SOIL

1. STICK 6–10 BRANCHES INTO THE SOIL

2. BIND TOGETHER WITH WIRE

3. STUFF IN FIR SPRIGS ALL THE WAY UP

"Mountain Bride" Chandelier

A sawed-off fir can be made into an unusual chandelier with a real "nature" feel. It should be a bit wild and bohemian.

You Need:

1 base of a Christmas tree, make sure that the branches are strong and evenly spaced

2 screw loops

1 strong leather strap

2 pieces of tissue paper, preferably blue and white

about 5 balance candle holders (see page 108) or about 5 squeeze holders for Christmas candles, found in craft stores

about 6 small red apples

about 5 small foil molds

about 5 Christmas candles (all depending on the number of branches)

wire

Remove small twigs and needles from the fir tree. Peel off the bark with a sharp knife. Shorten the branches.

Screw in the loops on the top and bottom of the sawed-off trunk and make sure that they are fastened securely. Thread the leather strap through the top loop and adjust the length to the height of the ceiling before tying the ends together.

Hang it from the ceiling to make it easier to work on. Place 2 pieces of tissue paper on top of each other. Pleat and cut into strips.

Fold it together at the top and attach to the bottom of the apples in the balance holders (see page 108) or under the squeeze holders if you're using those instead. Place a balance holder or a squeeze holder on each branch. Flatten the foil molds, cut crosses in the bottom, and slip over the candles to catch running wax. Place the candles in the holders. Thread a wire through an apple, attach it to the lower screw loop as a weight, and bend the end of the wire into a stop.

Adjust the weighting of the chandelier by moving the balance holders around on the branches.

Note: Remember that Christmas candles have a short burn time. Don't leave the room when the chandelier is lit!

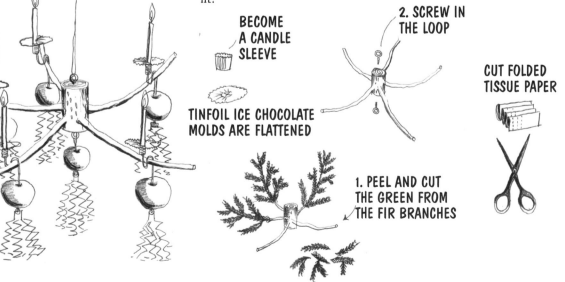

BECOME A CANDLE SLEEVE

2. SCREW IN THE LOOP

CUT FOLDED TISSUE PAPER

TINFOIL ICE CHOCOLATE MOLDS ARE FLATTENED

1. PEEL AND CUT THE GREEN FROM THE FIR BRANCHES

Balance Holders for Christmas Candles

Decorative and ingenious candle holder that decorates the Christmas tree. The apples function as plumb weights and can also be eaten. A fine point is that the candles stay straight even when the tree starts wilting.

You Need:
bendy but stable wire, about ¹⁄₁₆ inch thick
candle holders for Christmas candles (from craft stores)
small red apples
Christmas candles
optional: pleated, curled tissue paper (preferably white and blue)

Wrap the wire several times around the actual candle holder for stability. Use pliers if it gets difficult.

Make the wire into an S-shape about 1¼ inches from the holder.

The wire should then point down vertically. Thread an apple at the bottom of the wire and bend the end of the wire so the apple doesn't fall off.

The weight of the apple helps balance the candle holder on the branches. Put in the candles. If you want, pleat tissue paper and cut fringes to hang from the holders.

Be careful to place the holders away from any flammable materials.

Note: Remember never to walk away from a Christmas tree with real candles without putting them out. Despite all the warnings, it's really worth making these candle holders.

BALANCE HOLDER FOR CHRISTMAS LIGHTS

APPLE AS WEIGHT

BENDABLE, STABLE WIRE

CANDLE HOLDER FOR CHRISTMAS LIGHTS

THE WIRE IS WRAPPED AROUND THE CANDLE HOLDER

MAKE A BEND ABOUT 1¹⁄₄ INCHES FROM THE CANDLE HOLDER

Fruit Pyramid

I like edible decorations. We make this one every year. It can be made with several different kinds of fruit and is therefore suitable all year round. A fun going-away present.

You Need:
1 block of oasis (can be
    found in flower shops)
sprigs of fir
wooden skewers
kumquats
tangerines
small red apples
low plate or tray
mixed, unshelled nuts
    and/or whole Christmas
    spices

Cut the block of oasis into a cone shape. Insert fir sprigs in the bottom so the cone can stand stably.

Pierce the fruit with the wooden skewers and stick the other ends in the oasis cone. Work from the bottom up to the top. Poke in some sprigs of fir if the fruit doesn't cover everywhere.

Place on a plate or a tray and decorate with nuts and/or Christmas spices.

Slender Lingon Heart

Less is more. Very simple and incredibly decorative hung against a white wall.

You Need:
1 thick wire, bendable
sprigs of lingon
green binding thread

Bend the wire to a heart shape. Wind the ends around each other. Tie the lingon sprigs onto the wire one after the other with the binding thread. It should be very sparse. Hang on the wall.

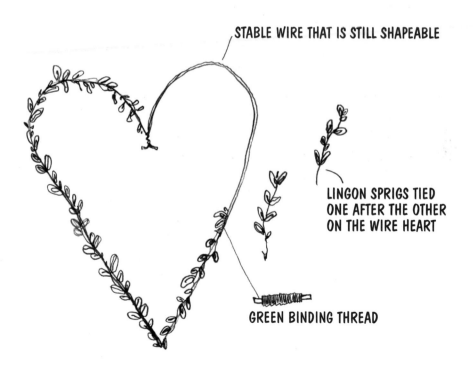

STABLE WIRE THAT IS STILL SHAPEABLE

LINGON SPRIGS TIED
ONE AFTER THE OTHER
ON THE WIRE HEART

GREEN BINDING THREAD

"SLENDER" LINGON HEART

Salt Candlestick

Super-easy candle holders that you make yourself out of any bowls. The candles can burn down; you don't need to worry about candle wax or the risk of fire. Perfect for candle stumps or on a long table where you need many candles. The salt also gives a soothing reminder of snow.

You Need:
transparent glasses or
    bowls
2–4 pounds regular salt
possibly 1 packet of bay
    leaves
possibly star anise
possibly cinnamon
candles

Fill the glasses or bowls with salt all the way up. If you want to, stick the spices down along the sides. Shove the candle into the center so it stands stable.

Tip: Make many and place them on a tray or along a long table.

Note: Never use sugar. It can catch fire.

SALT CANDLESTICK

BAY LEAVES AND STAR ANISE MAKE IT SMELL OF CHRISTMAS

GLASS BOWL WITH SALT AND A CANDLE

Fir Wreaths

I like straggly and bushy wreaths. They're even better with edible fruit. Ready-made straw frames make for stable wreaths.

You Need:
fir twigs
*ready-made straw wreaths
    (buy in craft stores or
    flower shops)*
green binding thread
small red apples
wire

Cut small twigs of fir. Place a few branches on the straw frame and, using the binding thread, tie the lower parts of the branches onto the frame. Continue until the entire frame is covered. Let the branches point a little here and there. It should look spontaneous, so don't be too careful.

Thread the apples on the wire and tie them to the wreath, either bunched together or evenly distributed across the wreath. Hang on the wall or your front door.

Tip: Citrus fruit is also a great addition to the wreath. You can also make fir garlands using the same method, with regular ropes as the frame.

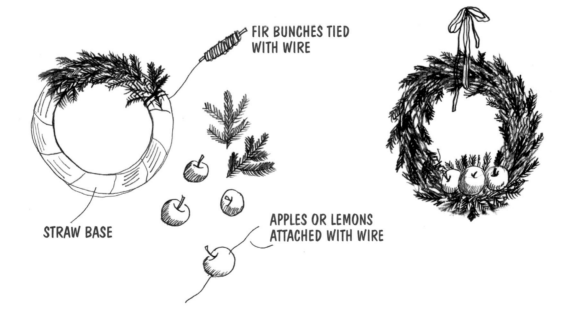

FIR BUNCHES TIED WITH WIRE

STRAW BASE

APPLES OR LEMONS ATTACHED WITH WIRE

Ernst's Wrapping School

As I get older, I care more and more about the ways my Christmas presents look, while their contents feel less important. I love having the presents lying under the Christmas tree where I can walk around and look at them. The trick of cutting folded paper is something I've been doing since I was a kid.

You Need:

wrapping paper, white or
    another neutral color

tape

1 blue paper

spray glue or other paper
    glue

Wrap your gift in the wrapping paper. Cut the blue paper to fit the package. Fold it in half. Cut out a pattern along the fold; draw it first if you feel uncertain. Make stars, hearts, or more advanced patterns, all according to your levels of ambition. Open up the paper. Attach to the wrapped gift using spray glue (best done outside) or other suitable paper glue.

Tip: Newspaper, old wallpaper, or corrugated paper are also great for wrapping Christmas presents. Kitchen appliances can be wrapped in a pretty new kitchen towel—2 presents in 1.

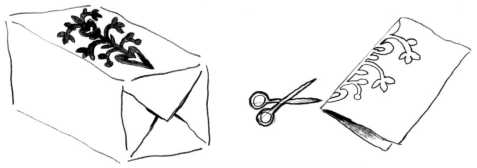

WHITE PRESENTS WITH BLUE PATTERNS

Citrus Decorations

Nothing smells as much like Christmas as citrus—nature's best Christmas decoration. Nowadays, you can find zesters in most kitchen appliance stores.

You Need:
lemons
oranges
possibly limes
zester

There aren't really any rules here. Make sure to choose fruit with fairly thick rinds and don't be afraid to mix different kinds. Limes can be a bit tricky because their rinds are thin, but the color combination looks great.

Then, using the coarse point of the zester, just freestyle patterns and serpentines on the rinds. Place in a bowl or on a pretty plate. Go ahead and leave the peel intact on some of the fruit—the mix is very appealing.

The fruits dry very quickly when you remove some of the rind. They're nice dried, too.

"Food and decoration go hand in hand. If I make a tomato soup, I might think of some upholstery fabric I want to design."

Ice Lanterns

The simplest and prettiest decorations in the world. All you need is a bucket and temperatures below freezing.

You Need:
1 regular plastic bucket,
   size optional
water
thick candles or tea lights

Fill the bucket with water. Place it outside in the cold overnight. Of course, it has to be below freezing for this to work . . .

The next day, the water has frozen, but not all the way through. Knock a hole on the top crust and pour out the water that hasn't frozen. Turn the bucket upside down and slide the rest of the ice out. Rinse with a bit of warm water if the ice won't come out of the bucket.

Place the ice lantern on the ground. Place the candle in the hole and light it.

Index

Big thanks to:
Julita Gård • Johanssons Blommor i Katrineholm • Julitaboden • Matlabbet, Ing-Britt och Inga • Klässbols Linneväveri

Also thanks to:
Familjen Karl-Arne Wagenius, Åsa Cederberg & Karl-Alfred in beautiful Funäsdalen and all the other nice people who have helped make this book.

Visit our website at www.skyhorsepublishing.com.

10 9 8 7 6 5 4 3

The Library of Congress has cataloged the hardcover edition as follows:
Kirchsteiger, Ernst.
Swedish Christmas traditions : a smorgasbord of Scandinavian recipes, crafts, and other holiday delights / by Ernst Kirchsteiger.
p. cm.
ISBN 978-1-61608-052-5 (hardcover : alk. paper)
1. Christmas cooking--Sweden. 2. Christmas decorations--Sweden. 3. Flower arrangement--Sweden. 4. Christmas--Sweden. I. Title.
TX739.2.C45K57 2010
394.266309485--dc22
2010029521

Cover design by Adam Bozarth

Paperback ISBN: 978-1-62914-419-1
Ebook ISBN: 978-1-62873-298-6

Printed in China

Translated by Ella Fitzsimmons

Recipes, flowers, decorations, and illustrations: Ernst Kirchsteiger
Text, food, and styling: Mia Gahne
Photos: Roland Persson
Graphic design: Torgny Karlsson
Creative consultant: Pelle Holm
Project leader: Ingela Holm